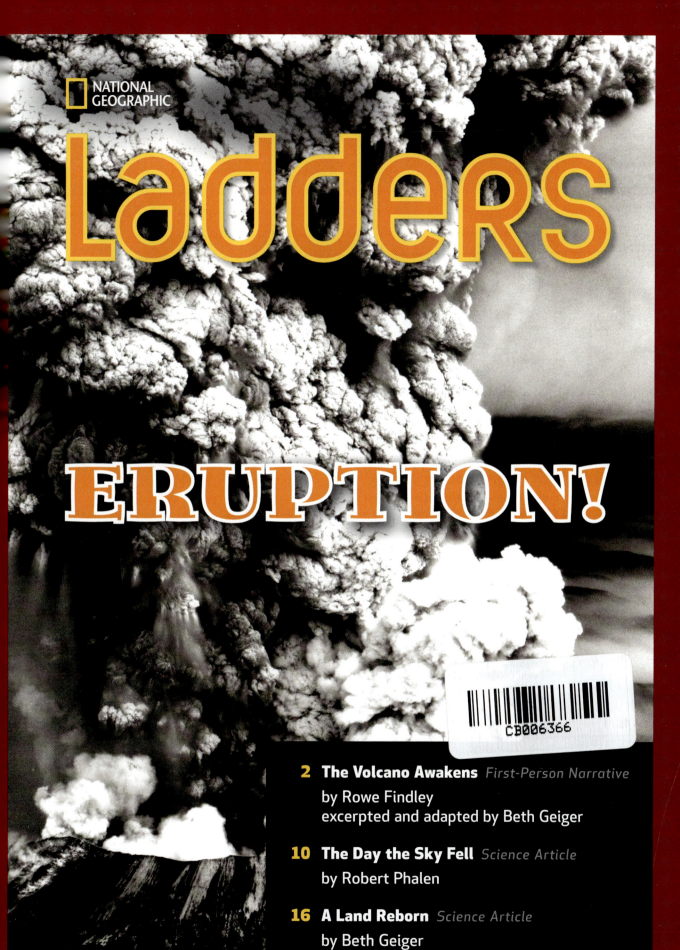

NATIONAL GEOGRAPHIC
Ladders

ERUPTION!

2 **The Volcano Awakens** *First-Person Narrative*
by Rowe Findley
excerpted and adapted by Beth Geiger

10 **The Day the Sky Fell** *Science Article*
by Robert Phalen

16 **A Land Reborn** *Science Article*
by Beth Geiger

24 **Discuss**

GENRE First-Person Narrative

Read to find out how the eruption of Mount St. Helens surprised scientists.

The Volcano Awakens

by Rowe Findley   excerpted and adapted by Beth Geiger

It is early Sunday morning, May 18, 1980. A phone call from my friend sends me rushing out of my hotel room to watch what's happening. Mount St. Helens is erupting!

I get into a helicopter for a better look. It is hard to accept what I see. The whole top of the mountain is gone. From its center, a column of ash shoots thousands of meters into the sky. Orange lightning flashes inside the black cloud of ash. The **eruption** goes on for more than nine hours.

NATIONAL GEOGRAPHIC ASSISTANT EDITOR

ROWE FINDLEY (1925–2003) joined National Geographic in 1959. He worked as an assistant editor for 31 years. Findley wrote a story on the 1980 Mount St. Helens eruption. It was the most popular story in the magazine's history. What was his assignment? Follow scientists as they study the volcano—no matter what happens!

We fly as close to the **volcano** as we dare. The thick ash makes it hard to breathe. All I see below us is a wasteland of hot, swirling ash. I soon learn that dozens of people are dead, and some of them are my friends.

For the past six weeks I have been living close to Mount St. Helens. Looking back, I must tell you that I feel lucky to be alive.

A column of ash, gas, and rock erupts from Mount St. Helens.

The volcano first began to wake up on March 16, when several small **earthquakes** shook the mountain. It was the first sign of activity in 123 years. Weeks later, jets of steam and ash erupted. That's when I decided to see the volcano for myself.

I met with residents and scientists after I arrived. I flew in helicopters, explored near the summit, and drove on remote roads to write about the volcano.

Earthquakes shook the mountain as melted rock and gases built up inside it. A fresh **crater** formed near the summit. Plus, the north side of the volcano was bulging and cracking. "This mountain is a powder keg," said David Johnston, a **geologist** from the United States Geological Survey (USGS).

One day, two geologists and I landed on the edge of the new crater. We were scooping up ash for testing. Softball-sized rocks that had been spit out of the crater were everywhere. It was like playing dodge ball with the volcano. I wanted to leave. It seemed as if the scientists were taking forever to collect their samples!

David Johnston enters the crater. He is getting samples. It's dangerous work. He has to watch out for flying rocks.

Mount St. Helens towers over Coldwater I, seen here on April 11, 1980. The camp is about 13 kilometers (8 miles) from the volcano.

Meanwhile, everyone watched Mount St. Helens. Sightseers flocked to the smoking volcano. They wanted to know what would happen, and when. But not even geologists knew for sure.

Officials formed a 16-kilometer (10-mile) "red zone" around the volcano. People were told to keep out of this area for their own safety. A man named Harry Truman refused to leave his home at Spirit Lake, which was inside the red zone. He had lived there for over 50 years. I visited his lodge to interview him. Truman said, "I get dozens of letters from children who worry about me. But I'm part of that mountain. I'm going to stay right here."

By late April, the explosions and ash eruptions quieted down. Yet a bulge on the north side of the mountain was still growing. Geologists were worried and puzzled.

The geologists needed to watch Mount St. Helens at all times, so they set up two camps several kilometers from the volcano. The camps were called Coldwater I and Coldwater II. The geologists believed the camps were a safe distance away. They were wrong.

Harry Truman and I shake hands at a school in Toutle, Washington. Students enjoyed listening to him talk about his love for the mountain.

Here is Coldwater I a few days after the eruption. You can see the top of Reid Blackburn's car. Reid, a photographer, did not survive the blast.

On Sunday, May 18, I watched the sun rise under clear skies. The mountain seemed calm. I saw no hint of what was about to happen.

Everything changed at 8:32 A.M. Geologists in Vancouver, Washington, received an urgent radio call from David Johnston at Coldwater II. "Vancouver, Vancouver, this is it!" he yelled. Those were his last words. The volcano exploded in a massive sideways blast. The blast destroyed everything for miles around, including both Coldwater camps. Johnston did not survive.

Campers flee from a cloud of super-hot gas, ash, and rock. It destroyed everything in its path. The man who took this picture barely escaped.

Now looking down from the helicopter, it seems as if we are on a different planet. Forests stood here just yesterday. Now the land is bare, lifeless, and buried under smoking ash. I think about how close I was to this dangerous mountain. It could have erupted while I was looking into the crater. I was very lucky, but some others were not.

Check In Why did Findley believe he was lucky to be alive?

GENRE Science Article   **Read to find out** about the effects of the eruption.

THE DAY
THE SKY
FELL

by Robert Phalen

A scientist points toward Mount St. Helens four weeks after the eruption. Rains have hardened the ash. The land is like a gray desert.

Volcanoes are a natural hazard. They can sleep for centuries and then suddenly wake up with a bang. During the Mount St. Helens **eruption,** the blast, mudflows, and ash cloud changed landscapes and lives.

THE BLAST An **earthquake** triggered the blast. As the mountain shook, the north face of the volcano crumbled. The largest **landslide** in recorded history tore down the side of Mount St. Helens. The landslide released the pressure that had built up inside the volcano. A massive explosion followed. It could be heard from 483 kilometers (300 miles) away.

The landslide had "uncorked" the volcano! A cloud of rocks, ash, volcanic gas, and steam shot out at airplane speeds. This was the blast cloud. It was searing hot and reached temperatures of 350°C (660°F)—hot enough to boil water and burn wood. The blast cloud fanned out over the land and snapped thousands of giant trees as if they were twigs.

In just minutes, the eruption destroyed more than 520 square kilometers (200 square miles) of forest. That's more land than the world's seven smallest countries put together. Twenty-six lakes and hundreds of kilometers of streams and rivers were wiped out. Millions of animals were killed. Fifty-seven people died, and many others barely escaped.

MUDFLOWS The small town of Toutle is located beside the North Fork Toutle River. Toutle is several kilometers downstream from Mount St. Helens. At first it seemed the town would be spared from the volcano. But this was not to be.

The huge landslide that "uncorked" the volcano dragged tons of ice down the mountain. The landslide stopped in the Toutle Valley, forming giant hills of boulders, soil, and buried ice. Hot ash from the eruption quickly melted the ice. Tons of water then mixed with the ash, soil, and rock. It was a recipe for disaster.

This hot, smelly mixture surged down the Toutle Valley toward the town. Like giant baseball bats, hundreds of tree trunks swirled in the thick, muddy water. Mudflows such as these are called lahars. Lahars are part flood, part mud and ash. They destroy everything in their path. Authorities raised the alarm. Helicopters were sent in to get people out.

The lahar was only minutes away by the time the last people were rescued. All of Toutle's residents were saved, but their homes were not. Smaller lahars occurred elsewhere around the volcano. That day lahars destroyed 27 bridges and more than 200 homes.

A house lies buried in mud near Toutle, Washington. The mud is as thick as wet cement.

RAINING ASH The volcanic eruption shot a column of ash 19 kilometers (12 miles) into the sky. The ash blew eastward. Within hours, cities hundreds of kilometers away were in complete darkness. People reported seeing a black curtain of ash cover the sky and block the sun. Dangerous lightning filled the skies. Then the ash fell like a dark blizzard.

In some places it was so dark people couldn't see their own hands. Stores closed and traffic stopped. Travelers took shelter in schools and gas stations.

Volcanic ash is not powdery like regular ash. It's made of tiny pieces of glass and rock. As the ash rained down, it killed insects and birds. It also damaged crops. Breathing was difficult. People covered their faces to protect themselves. Car engines choked on the ash and stopped running.

It took weeks to clean up. An incredible amount of ash erupted on that day. If all the ash were piled onto a football field, the pile would be 241 kilometers (150 miles) tall. It would reach into space!

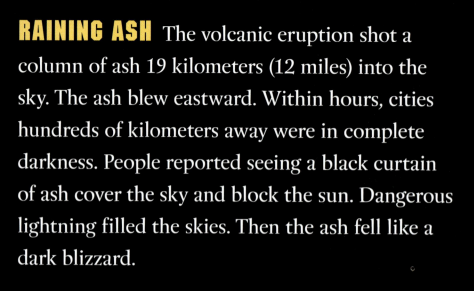

Workers drive snowplows to remove the ash from this road in Yakima, Washington. But the ash kept falling. The town was in total darkness by 9:30 A.M.

Check In How did the eruption affect people nearby?

15

GENRE Science Article

Read to find out how life is returning around Mount St. Helens.

A Land Reborn

by Beth Geiger

The 1980 eruption of Mount St. Helens killed millions of birds, small animals, fish, and insects. Thousands of large animals such as elk also died. Vast forests were erased in seconds.

That massive **eruption** was disastrous to life nearby. For scientists, the eruption has been a rare chance to observe how life starts anew.

◁ U.S. Forest Service scientist Charlie Crisafulli

Before the eruption, the forests around Mount St. Helens were rooted in rich soil. In an instant, the eruption buried the soil, valleys, and bodies of water under tons of burning-hot ash and rock.

How has nature recovered since 1980? Scientists such as Charlie Crisafulli of the United States Forest Service have been watching closely. The land around Mount St. Helens is coming back to life. "Nature is tough," says Crisafulli.

BLAST ZONE This area was destroyed by the eruption. It covers 370 square kilometers (143 square miles). Its farthest point from the volcano is 27 kilometers (17 miles) away.

SPIRIT LAKE Almost nothing survived in Spirit Lake. Rock, ash, and dead trees filled the lake. Bacteria soon made the water toxic.

PUMICE PLAIN This section of the blast zone was closest to the volcano. Nothing survived. The land was just a bare stretch of pumice. Pumice is rock that forms when lava cools quickly.

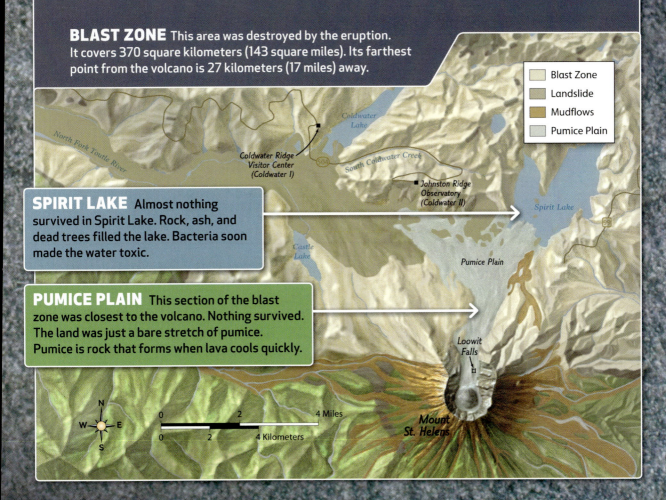

17

The Blast Zone

Imagine miles of dead trees, all flattened in the same direction. That's what the blast did to the forest north of Mount St. Helens. "It went from a vertical forest to a horizontal forest," says Charlie Crisafulli. Up to 1 meter (3 feet) of ash covered the ground in the blast zone.

This thick layer of volcanic ash was nasty stuff at first. It was burning hot, and it smothered many plants and animals. But in the long term, the ash will add nutrients to the soil.

Amazingly, some life survived. Tadpoles survived beneath the ice in frozen ponds. Gophers that were hibernating in their burrows survived. Some plants and seeds were protected by pockets of deep snow.

1980

SUPER SURVIVORS

Crisafulli says the surviving plants have grown like crazy. "We were surprised to see patches of green that very first summer. Now some cottonwood trees are already 18 meters (59 feet) tall," he says.

Gophers live underground. Many survived the blast. Today gophers are one of the commonest mammals in the area.

Gophers still rule the roost underground. "You can hardly walk without falling into a gopher hole," says Crisafulli. Gophers churn the soil as they dig. This makes it easier for plants to take hold. Plus, decomposing trees help make the soil more fertile.

2011

Pumice Plain

Before it was called the pumice plain, a towering old forest grew up the north slope of the **volcano.** Crystal clear streams weaved between giant trees. The forest was home to countless animals.

After May 18, 1980, "The pumice plain bore no resemblance to its former self," says Crisafulli. Gases reached 704°C (1,300°F) over part of this area. That's hot enough to melt soda cans. All life was quickly erased. Then the land was buried under ash and pumice.

The pumice plain covered 39 square kilometers (15 square miles) of the blast zone. "This was the newest rock in the world. With very little life, it was also very quiet," says Crisafulli.

1980

WATERWORKS   Water has reshaped the pumice plain. Its once-smooth slope now has gorges and a canyon. It might normally take centuries for streams to carve such deep gorges. But the **landslide** and the eruption dropped thick layers of loose material. Melting ice and snow formed streams that carried away the loose material. This process formed the features you see in the pumice plain today.

Loowit Falls spills down the mountain. The stream flows over the pumice plain. It formed this canyon in just ten years.

Spiders and insects arrived first, carried by the wind. After they died, their decaying bodies helped create tiny patches of new soil. Elk droppings provided seeds. Crisafulli says the pumice plain now looks more green than gray. In summer, meadows display colorful flowers such as purple lupines. Birds, grasshoppers, and frogs fill the air with their sounds.

2004

Spirit Lake

Spirit Lake used to be scenic. The eruption changed that. Ash, pumice, and dead trees filled the lake, which was inside the blast zone. This material raised the water level 61 meters (200 feet). Thousands of dead trees floated on the surface. Only bacteria survived. "It smelled like rotten eggs," says Crisafulli.

1980

UNDERWATER FOREST Dead trees still cover one-fifth of Spirit Lake. The land around it is stark.

But under water is a different story. "It's like an underwater forest," Crisafulli reports. Sunken trees and aquatic plants make great habitats for insects and snails.

Surprisingly, trout swim by. How did fish get into the lake? Crisafulli thinks someone snuck them in around 1991. It's too bad, because ecologists had hoped to study how Spirit Lake changed on its own.

A heron flies overhead, and mayflies swarm over the lake. Crisafulli says that in about 300 years, the area around Mount St. Helens might look as it did before the eruption. At least it might until the next time the volcano blows its top.

2009

Check In How is life returning to the different areas in the blast zone?

23

Discuss

1. Describe some of the ways in which Mount St. Helens connects the three pieces in this book.

2. How well does Findley communicate the danger he was in? Use the text to support your answer.

3. Choose one event in "The Day the Sky Fell." Describe what caused the event and how it changed Earth's surface.

4. What do you think is the most important idea in "A Land Reborn"? What makes you think that? Use the text to support your answer.

5. What else would you like to know about Mount St. Helens? How could you find out more?